Weddings in Italy

Angelo Garini · Enzo Miccio

Weddings in Italy

Stewart Tabori & Chang
New York

Published in 2009 by Stewart, Tabori & Chang
An imprint of ABRAMS

First published by Mondadori Electa S.p.A. 2008 Milan

Library of Congress Cataloging-in-Publication Data
Garini, Angelo.
  [Matrimonio chei vorrei. English]
  Weddings in Italy / Angelo Garini and Enzo Miccio.
      p. cm.
  "First Published by Mondadori Electa S.p.A. 2008 Milan."
  "English translation ... [by] Mondadori Electa S.p.A."
  ISBN 978-1-58479-796-8
  1. Weddings—Italy—Pictorial works. I. Miccio, Enzo. II. Title.
  HQ745.G3313 2009
  395.2'2—dc22
2009007176

Text by Angelo Garini
Art Director: Giorgio Seppi
Editor: Lidia Maurizi
Graphic design: Federico Magi
Graphic coordination: Francesca Rossi
Layouts: Elisa Seghezzi
Editing: Lucia Moretti
Picture research: Irene Giannini
English translation: Jay Hyams
English-language typesetting: William Schultz

Stewart, Tabori & Chang books are available at special discounts when pur-
chased in quantity for premiums and promotions as well as fundraising
or educational use. Special editions can also be created to specification.
For details, contact specialmarkets@hnabooks.com or the address below.

Printed and bound in Spain
10 9 8 7 6 5 4 3 2 1

HNA
harry n. abrams, inc.
a subsidiary of La Martinière Groupe

115 West 18th Street
New York, NY 10011
www.hnabooks.com

Contents

Introduction

The pages of this book will take you on a photographic journey to some of the most beautiful landscapes of Italy. These are the locales that provided us with the opportunity to conceive a new way of celebrating the wedding event—a worthy project since the symbolic significance of the wedding ceremony has changed greatly over the course of recent years. Once seen as the all-important step taken by a bride and groom in their passage toward independence from their families, it has increasingly become a much-anticipated occasion to unite the family members and friends dearest to the bride and groom.

This of course in no way diminishes the excitement of the event—it remains timeless, always full of emotion. In recognizing the union of two people, a wedding encompasses overwhelming happiness, enjoyment, and festivities in which the bride and groom will begin their roles as the leading players in a long-cherished dream. It is the one day when everything must be perfect and, most of all, unique and surprising for those taking part.

The starting place during our initial meeting with a bride and groom is precisely that: a quest for novel and exciting ideas, suggestions, or proposals to help us create an unexpected wedding event. Our guiding philosophy—the one behind every new undertaking—is to activate the imagination.

Each project begins with deciding where the ceremony will be performed and where the reception will take place.

It is then necessary to identify an idea, atmosphere, color, or special element that, whether suggested by the location itself or, even better, a passion shared by the couple, can be adopted as the event's primary theme. Study of the open-air settings and the interior spaces influences the selection of furnishings, scenographic illumination, and floral decorations.

Our intention is always to establish harmony among the event's many elements. As the occasion requires, designs for decorative structures are devised, custom fabrics sought out, and beautiful objects collected to contribute to the overall effect.

A guest's first impression of a wedding is the invitation. Its design should correspond to the style that will be elaborated throughout the event; it should match the printing style of the program, the menu, and the place cards.

Another extremely important element is the soundtrack, the audible frame for the various steps of the event, adding emotional depth to each. This begins with the ceremony, for which the classical repertory always takes precedence, and concludes with the cutting of the cake, which, as the prelude to the party that will follow, calls instead for something more contemporary.

Color themes also carry emotional weight and are introduced in the floral compositions that decorate the site chosen for the ceremony, whether this is a church, garden gazebo, or city hall. The same range of colors—perhaps enriched by stronger tonalities—will also be applied to the decorations for the reception area.

And the tables? The tables are always elaborate, set with napkins in the colors of the wedding and surrounded by place settings that vary according to the chosen theme and the desired historical references. Laden with flowers and candles, the tables create a different effect depending upon their shape—round, square, or, where possible, long banquet tables. While the dinner should move along briskly, it must not be rushed; the service must be impeccable and the menu should be attentive to seasonal availability and local produce. Which brings us, then, to the final celebratory moment of the wedding—the cutting of the cake. The cake itself should be large, impressive, exquisite, and the moment should gather everyone around the newlyweds for the toasts that mark the beginning of the party and the dancing.

We have sought to relate all of the above in this book, illustrating in particular several weddings we have "staged" during our professional career. Many of these events were challenges, even adventures, but that only increased our enthusiasm. We will tell the story of a wedding on a lake, a splendid backdrop in northern Italy where a private island became, for one night, the setting for the dancing of a thousand fairies; a wedding in the countryside, set in the hall of an antique convent with strong mystical suggestions; a wedding in the elaborate space of the foyer of the opera house of Ferrara, which, in an extraordinary gesture, was made available for a pair of opera lovers. Then we have gone through the seasons of the year with weddings in winter or under the warm sun of Salento, where the gardens of an antique ducal palace were opened and brought to new life for the occasion. Due homage is paid to Venice, with two weddings, one that saw the couple celebrating with their guests for several days in sites and palaces full of historic import. The sea served as the stage on which magical events took place at Portofino, Naples, and Ravello. Mountains watched over ceremonies that took place at Bormio and Alagna, while the hilly landscapes of Tuscany, from Lucca to Siena to the greenery of Chianti, added a further touch of beauty with their unmistakable panoramas.

Every one of these weddings realized a dream. Together with each couple who turned to us, we followed the particular route to the realization of their vision, considering even the smallest details. Listening to and interpreting the desires of the bride and the groom, we had the pleasure and honor of sharing a time of great importance and happiness in their lives—and also in the story of their love.

Angelo Garini • Enzo Miccio

Romantic atmospheres

*T*he couple want a wedding that will be truly unique, emotional, and rounded off with an unforgettable evening. The search for a worthy location leads to an extraordinary corner of Italy, a place suspended in the air over the Gulf of Tigullio. In the past it was a convent, and even today its evocative atmosphere induces the quiet contemplation of the enchanting scenery below. This very particular space, which hides a cloister with an open arcade on two sides, is framed by splendid Italian gardens with a courtyard of wisteria, camellias, and tangerine trees. A romantic setting: The names of the flowers alone suggest the rare enchantment of the place.

In a landscape like this, so full of the fascination of history and the colors of exuberant nature, it seems impossible to select a color theme that would exalt the background rather than clashing with it. For this reason preference is given to white, a fine counterpoint to the intense blue of the sky and the sea, and also to gold, capable of emphasizing and embellishing the richness of the classical architecture. The couple want an open-air ceremony, and the most appropriate setting is the cloister; they will take their vows at the center of the garden. The ancient wellhead in the middle of the space becomes a secular altar on which to rest the wedding registers amid floral compositions and candles. The guests take up places in the arcades or watch from seats on the surrounding low walls, supplied with colored cushions for the occasion. Following the ceremony, everyone moves to the grand terrace alongside the convent. The incomparable view of the Gulf of Tigullio, shining in the late-afternoon light, welcomes the guests in its wide embrace as they enjoy cocktails.

Sunset, with its serene and relaxed atmosphere, is accompanied by the sound of jazz. Dinner takes place on another natural stage, an enchanted corner of the splendid gardens overlooking the sea. With nightfall, the tables are illuminated by candlelight, inventing a landscape that contrasts with that of the surrounding coastline, punctuated by thousands of lights. The lapping of waves in the background, the fresh night air, the happy toasts and laughter become the romantic frame that prepares for the moment of the cutting of the cake.

The cake, an elegant architecture of gold icing, awaits the newlyweds on the uppermost terrace. And while toasts are offered, the final poetic note is dedicated to the sea, where thousands of torches appear floating on the waves.

The last, skilled adjustment to the bride's gown. The nuptials take place against the splendid background of the Gulf of Tigullio, pearl of the Ligurian Sea, amid nineteenth-century architecture and the Italian garden that hosts the ceremony.

For the all-important "I do," the bride has chosen to hold a romantic bouquet of antique roses that blend the soft shades of pale lavender with the warmer notes of apricot.

The cloister is ready for the exchange of rings. The bride and groom will meet in the middle, at the ancient wellhead, which for this occasion has been turned into an altar.

The guests will watch from beneath the arcades decorated with spheres and garlands of asparagus fern, roses, lisianthus, and tulips (below).

White rose petals have been strewn along the route to be taken by the bride (opposite). The ceremony is accompanied by the sweet music of a harp.

The floral decoration, of rare elegance, blends the soft form of the cascading composition spilling from the wellhead with the rigid shapes of the four uprights that terminate in white spheres of roses and lisianthus (right and below).

There are also the flowers that seem to burst out of soft sacks of pale lilac silk, located on small round tables (opposite).

Bonbonnière gift boxes for the guests are set up on a table under a pergola shaded by an age-old wisteria. A sweet surprise is hidden inside the silk boxes, which are arranged to alternate with small bouquets and candles.

The tabletops are completely covered by mirrors that multiply the lights of the candles and the glinting shine of the crystal. At the center are bouquets of lisianthus, roses, and clouds of baby's breath.

The color gold enhances and emphasizes the mirror reflections. The menu is written in gold letters, the ribbon that holds it to the napkin is gold, and so is the delightful heart that seals the connection. The votive candleholders on the tables are gold, as are many of the other decorative details.

In the darkness on the terrace overlooking the sea, the shimmering flames of the candles on the tables contribute to the enchantment of this convivial moment.

A short walk beneath a leafy pergola leads to the terrace where the cake has been placed. The route is given fairy-tale dreaminess by candles suspended in lanterns, in floral garlands, and along the walls that mark the path.

And suddenly there is the cake, decorated
with masterful skill, peeking from a cloud-like wrap-
ping of tulle.

In the heart of town

No doubts, no location scouting: This wedding will take place in Tuscany, on the splendid estate of the groom's family. The home is unique, surrounded by a tiny ancient town, originally fortified, located between Florence and Siena. The ceremony will be held in a church nestled amid an expanse of olive trees with vineyards stretching across the countryside to the horizon.

The future newlyweds, very young, wish to make their wedding into a festival, given the presence of so many of their friends, who will be lodged for the event in the homes of the small town. Our plans begin with the church—how can a setting so unique and evocative be made even more special? Our proposed solution delights the couple: We will bring the power of the splendid and luxuriant exterior landscape into the mystical space inside. Sacred and profane blend—unexpectedly, the fields and age-old olive trees step across the threshold and, as though by magic, cover the floor and fill the arcades. The only furnishings left inside are the simple and spare prie-dieu and the pews, which will accommodate only the closest family members. The guests will witness the ceremony standing, as was the

*The final touches to the
bride's gown are entrusted
to her mother.*

case in the oldest liturgy, and form a close embrace around the newlyweds.
In the half-light of the interior, the glow of the many candles placed in the
original iron candleholders will stand out even more.

As for the reception, divided into the traditional steps of cocktails,
dinner, and the cutting of the cake, the magnificent terraced garden offers
the perfect setting. Abundantly blooming rambling roses outline and
soften the sober façades of the old stone constructions, which also contrast
with the décor of flowers and olive trees arranged among the dinner tables.
A transparent tent makes possible a view of the medieval town of Volpaia,
where the play of lights emphasizes the structure of the castle. By then it
is evening and lights are coming on in the highest terraces overlooking the
villa, the site for the cutting of the cake, itself a masterpiece of the
confectioner's art.

The moment then arrives when the doors of the deconsecrated church
known as the Commenda are thrown open. Fitted with a modern sound
system, for one entire night it will witness the music and dancing of the
many friends who have traveled here to celebrate with the couple.

The guests in morning dress and top hats await the arrival of the bride on the grounds of the church, with its beautiful carpet of grass flanked by olive trees.

The interior of the church, no longer walled off from
nature, is completely covered by a grassy carpet
on which groups of olive trees have been placed.
The vases of the trees are wrapped in canvas, and
the only illumination comes from the twinkling
light of candles, creating a soft, serene atmosphere.

Placed at the church's exit, a large wicker basket, interwoven with garlands of honeysuckle and viburnum, supplies guests with packets of petals—a variation on the traditional throwing of the rice (below).

*The guests will enjoy cocktails, sitting on comfortable sofas
set up amid the flowering geraniums and lemon trees
on the terraces of the family villa in the
medieval town of Volpaia.*

And the sugared almonds, which are the all-important
wedding favor and most traditional symbol of an
Italian wedding? They are offered on a table
elaborately decorated with precious antique pieces
of French glass, silver, and Tuscan bronzes.

Dinner will be served in the rose garden, under a transparent covering. The centerpieces on the tables call for grouping objects of varying shape and color on mirrors to reflect the light of the many candles.

The wedding cake is the symbol chosen to decorate the cover of the menu. It also appears as the background to the list of dishes to be served.

The cake is a spectacular construction for which every decorative element is made of chocolate and icing. It looks like a series of marzipan baskets containing dozens of roses; these were made and colored by hand, perfectly simulating compositions made with real flowers.

The final moment of the dinner finds the guests, emotionally moved, taking part in the cutting of the cake.

Exquisite icing roses blend with the real rose petals that form the carpet on which the cake rests.

A celebration within the celebration. At the end of the reception, cascades of fireworks flare at the moment the cake is cut. The guests stand in the garden to watch the pyrotechnical display in honor of the newlyweds.

A terrace on the sea

*A*precious stone set high on the magnificent Amalfi coast—
such is Ravello, the location chosen by this young couple
for their wedding. The celebration will take place between the pristine
white cathedral and the spectacular park of Villa Cimbrone, with its dense
greenery and flowers overlooking the sea. The couple wishes to turn the
various moments of the day into separate situations, alternating flowers,
colors, and music. There is also a secret request from the groom: He
wants to surprise his bride, to crown the festivities somehow, creating a
moment of great emotion. To satisfy such desires, the ceremony and the
reception, the sacred moment and the convivial one, the cathedral and the
villa, different and contrasting situations, will blend into a single plan that
takes place in the streets of the small town, which the couple and their
guests will travel on foot.

On a warm afternoon in early summer, the cathedral's simple,
immaculate façade dazzles in the sunlight. Inside, the crowd awaits the
arrival of the couple. In the shadowy interior, the magnificent fourteenth-
century marble pulpit, covered with decorations, stands out, and the floor
has been left bare to reveal all its beauty. At the end of the ceremony, the

guests will walk along the narrow streets, through covered passages, and up long stairways, to arrive at the villa garden. Formerly the summer residence of a family of English nobles, it is now used exclusively for special events. Another long stroll, this time beneath ancient pines, with views of the Gulf of Sorrento, leads to the "terrace of sighs," a magical place surrounded by ancient sculptures. This is the setting for cocktails, with music provided by guitarists and a soprano. Later, in the so-called crypt, an area like a loggia looking out over the sea, dinner is served beneath neo-Gothic arches to the accompaniment of piano music.

The place chosen for the cutting of the cake is the pavilion of the tea house, a fantastic construction that unites Moorish notions with Gothic forms in a splendor of antique local ceramics. After toasts are made to their happiness, the newlyweds begin the dancing, but just then the garden suddenly comes to bright life. A crescendo of music that seems to come from the trees themselves—the branches, flowers, bushes, all of it— joins a dance of light that, with perfect timing, brings to a conclusion this unforgettable day, to the delighted amusement of the bride.

Baby's breath and roses dominate the floral decorations. Tiny white inflorescences of Ammi majus are well suited for the bride's hair and also blend well with the colorful roses. Both white and lilac-colored Ammi majus embrace the rich peony blossoms that make up the wedding bouquet.

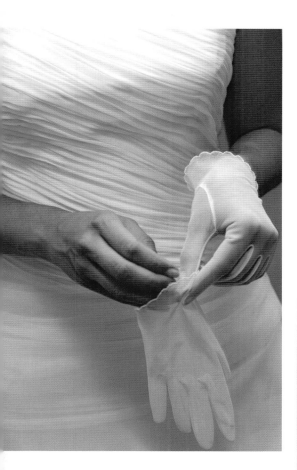

Small baskets of white baby's breath have been placed along the streets of Ravello as well as in the cathedral where the religious rite will take place. A carpet of white petals awaits the arrival of the bride.

The cathedral of Ravello, with its severe beauty, is decorated with a route marked off by tall structures completely covered with baby's breath and illuminated by small candles.

Through the characteristic covered passages of Ravello, the bride and groom and their guests reach the reception site, Villa Cimbrone, splendidly overlooking the Gulf of Sorrento.

The guests are welcomed to the wonderful "terrace of sighs" by marble busts arranged like silent guardians, each with its ivy crown.

The panoramic view from the outermost tip of the spur on which Ravello stands is considered among the most beautiful in Italy.

After cocktails, the wedding party will move to the cloister, the oldest part of the villa.

The dinner takes place in the crypt, distinguished by elegant arcades that open out over the view. Each table is decorated with roses of a different color wrapped around a curling piece of gilt wire.

The series of arcades, the overarching ribs, and the rough texture of the materials make the place almost solemn, but at the same time it is full of fairy-tale suggestions. The menu is printed on a watercolor design that features the roses used in the decorations (bottom).

*In a stroke of inspired scenography,
the cake shines magically from inside
the tea house pavilion.*

*The cake is an explosion of hearts that seem to swirl in the
air around the iced structure. Hanging from the beams
of the pavilion are small candlelit lanterns.*

Tribute to the opera

The chosen church is the ninth-century abbey of Pomposa, a splendid Romanesque jewel about thirty miles east of Ferrara. Also highly original is the location for the reception: the opera house of Ferrara, a site layered with history and art. The choice of music as the connecting thread for the project seems immediately natural. The ceremony will take place in the church of Santa Maria, which is part of the Benedictine abbey. It glows with the force of its austere architecture but is also integrated into the nature of the *lidi* of Ferrara—the beaches along the Adriatic—which surround it. The interior is an explosion of color: Fourteenth-century frescoes cover the walls and contrast with the bicolor design of the mosaic floor. Thus, we decide to emphasize the pictorial decoration with floral compositions that repeat and exalt the colors. The couple have chosen to include the rite of coronation in their nuptial ceremony—while exchanging their vows, they will crown each other with garlands woven of ivy and ribbons. All this will take place to the accompaniment of an orchestra and operatic voices—every step of the evening will be an homage to music.

At the conclusion of the ceremony, the guests will move to the splendid foyer of the Ferrara opera house. The gold and ivory decoration of the eighteenth-century wood paneling, the ceiling frescoes, the antique crystal-pendant chandeliers, the velvet divans, all conspire to create an atmosphere of rare suggestion. And a treat awaits the guests: During cocktails, as they are comfortably seated in the theater boxes, a ballet will be performed just for them, a leap backward in time to the age when court theaters often gave performances for a few privileged guests.

Dinner is to be served in halls facing the Este ducal palace. The menu is a modern version of the rich courses once prepared in that castle. Music is still the lead player; a soprano sings famous arias to the accompaniment of a piano. The cake, resplendent with its golden musical-staff decorations, is the final act of a truly theatrical reception. It appears with a flourish and brings this operatic wedding to a close.

A formal wedding means the groom wears morning dress, in this case completed with a top hat (right); the bride has chosen a romantic gown enriched by dense embroidery (below).

The basilica of Santa Maria in the abbey of Pomposa is a splendid example of Romanesque art, its interior decorated with polychrome frescoes. Two sets of stairs connect the raised altar to the area where the couple will be seated. Frescoes by Vitale da Bologna (opposite) dominate the setting.

The couple have decided to personalize the ceremony by inserting the rite of coronation. Two ivy garlands are prepared (above), which the bride and groom will place on each other's heads. Pale rose petals have been scattered on the white-and-black mosaic paving (top).

The basilican church, with a nave and two aisles, has a cycle of fourteenth-century frescoes by the Bologna school, including depictions of stories from the Old and New Testaments and scenes of the Apocalypse (right).

Flower balls made with interwoven branches of Pittosporum *are decorated with spirals of roses, tulips, carnations, and berries of* Hypericum *in colors inspired by the warm tones of the frescoes.*

In a highly unusual gesture, the opera house of Ferrara is made available for the reception. The bride, wearing a dress with truly theatrical accents, looks down at the stage, where later a special performance will take place.

A row of gilt-wood candlestands illuminates the table on which the boxes of sugared almonds are arranged.

The main hall glows with the light of antique lamps. On each table is a composition of candlestands with beautiful bobeches (drip catchers) and white and pink flowers (opposite).

Music is the theme of the event, and in its honor, each table bears
a small piece of sheet music with a few bars of a famous operatic aria.
During dinner the guests will be entertained by a soprano singing
several selections.

The wedding cake is decorated with musical
staffs and notes written in gold, which stand
out against the pale icing.

A fairy-tale island

A young couple, but demanding. They want to amaze their many guests. During the search for the ideal location, various possibilities are put forward, and in the end the desire for a place that can truly surprise takes us in the direction of a setting that is already part of a dream: an island! Lake Garda fulfills the wish with a private island that also happens to possess the ancient palace of a noble family. This home, a personal interpretation of the architecture of the Venetian palazzo, stands atop a spur of rock above a play of terraces and Italian gardens sloping down toward the expanse of the lake. Much of the island is an English-style park, which extends all the way to the water. Flocks of herons stop here on their way across the lake—this is the place for the couple's wedding. The church is on the coast, small and secluded on a hill overlooking the lake and almost submerged in the surrounding woods.

Meetings with the couple begin, the goal being to establish the themes of the wedding. The bride wants her gown to be designed especially for her; with this in mind, we seek inspiration in the sumptuous court gowns of the eighteenth century, which serve as the departure point for the

creation of the final design. Nature soon takes a hand in the plans too, with the motif of the flowering tree becoming the connecting theme. Thus, having entered the church, the bride will make her way to the altar beneath a series of vaults formed by trees draped with pale pink and white roses.

After the ceremony, the bride and groom cross the water by antique motorboat and arrive at the "island of the fairies," as it is called for the occasion. Cocktails are served on the palace's panoramic terrace. At dinnertime, the couple and their guests are led along garden paths toward the opposite end of the island, where a large pavilion has been set up in a wooded glade. Each table is decorated by a tree draped with flowers. Only when the time comes for the cake is the most magical spot on the island revealed. At that all-important moment, the woods seem to fill with fairies that fly off the tree branches and surround the newlyweds. And while the cake is cut, the lake lights up in the bursts of a spectacular fireworks display that crowns an enchanted wedding.

The interior of the church where the ceremony will take place has been transformed into a small forest of green trees draped with polyantha roses. The antique tile flooring has been left bare to create greater contrast with the floral decoration (opposite).

The bride, romantically wrapped in a cloud of tulle, holds a bouquet of roses with enormous corollas in full bloom.

When they leave the church, the newlyweds are driven to a waiting motorboat in a rare antique automobile of which only two examples exist.

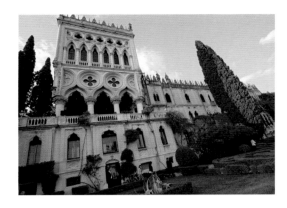

For the wedding the place has assumed the name "island of the fairies." Fairies have clearly inspired the menu, since they can be seen resting atop it as though briefly interrupting their flight.

Melitea

Lurikeen

Flooriloo

Deepysleepy

Emiliano e Giorgia

Set with silver chairs, the tables are decorated with large trees full of flowers displaying the same pink tonalities as the tablecloths.

The trees are illuminated by the light of many small candles.

The bonbonnière table—the keepsake chosen as a memento of this wedding is a small silk box that contains a jewel hidden among the traditional sugared almonds.

In a deliberate contrast with the old-fashioned structure of the palace, the park has been decorated with elements of modern design.

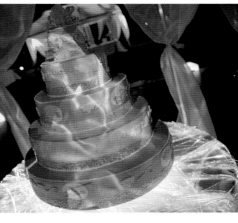

For the cutting of the cake, a gazebo has been set up in a glade in the woods; inside, many small fairies fly about, which the guests can keep as souvenirs of the day.

A celebration with angels

The bride collects angels, in all shapes and kinds, a passion shared by her future husband. The two of them have chosen her family home in the countryside of Lucca for the celebration of their wedding. The house, a beautiful example of restructured rural architecture, stands at the bottom of a group of tree-covered hills. The large, almost completely level garden that surrounds it is framed by a long row of typical Tuscan cypresses.

These broad vistas free the imagination, leading to the idea of a celebration taking advantage of the many available angles opening onto different views of the surrounding landscape.

The church chosen for the wedding ceremony stands atop one of the hills surrounding the property, and it enjoys a splendid view of the valley. Many other churches are equally close and boast artistic values; this one has been selected because of its frescoes, which feature angels and cherubs in various styles.

A striking work of trompe l'oeil painted drapery that seems to frame the apse suggests the idea of decorating the arches and side chapels with

The painted fabric drapery on the sides of the apse was the inspiration for the floor-length silk draperies that decorate the church, along with an alternation of garlands of ivy, asparagus fern, and Ruscus. White and green are the dominant colors in the church.

silk draperies of the same color. This baroque touch is very much in accordance with the period of the church's construction.

Baroque ornamentation becomes the dominant theme, further developed in the decorative ribbons and festoons that cover almost all the side vaults in a soft design with an antique sensibility.

The reception, set up in the villa's garden, is enlivened by a string orchestra positioned in a small outdoor theater. Cocktails, served among luxuriant beds of lavender, antique roses, and potted lemon trees, is prelude to the dinner, for which two long banquet tables have been prepared.

The frescoed angels and cherubs in the church paid homage to the bride's special passion, and this continues with the decoration of the tables, which include a collection of antique glasses with etched images of angels. The tablecloths are green, in pale sage tones, with accents of bright lavender partly supplied by the large bunches of that flower used in the decorations. Just as in a fable, "as night falls on the edge of the forest" a bonfire is lit and the chefs set up their grill. At the end of dinner, the cutting of the cake brings the newlyweds and their guests to the pool. Floodlights come on and illuminate the couple, standing with their cake beneath an old wooden portico, behind them a background of stone. In that moment, as though by magic, hundreds of small flames are lit along the branches of the trees all around.

Two long banquet tables have been set up for the guests in the garden, with the hills of the Lucca countryside in the background.

The decoration alternates shades of green and lilac in a harmony of roses, lavender, Ammi majus, mulberries, and Hypericum.

Flowers and berries in containers made of moss and leaves alternate with candles specially made in the color of the roses.

The colors of the long tables alternate between the lavender silk and the sage linen. The napkins are wrapped with taffeta ribbons.

81

Groups of large, luminous globes float in the pool, rising and falling with the movement of the water.

A small tent made of fabric and draped with colored ribbons is ready to welcome the wedding cake, which will be cut against the background of the pool.

The cake, the final surprise of the day, also presents the theme colors,
the same that have led all the chromatic decisions. The petals of small
pale lilac flowers open against a background of green icing.

The colors of winter

A wedding in the heart of winter, steeped in the season's foggy, rarefied atmosphere. A wedding whose themes exalt snow, ice, and everything that is white and silver. This is the bride's request. Stimulating and unusual, the theme presents numerous possibilities. We begin with a study of the site, or rather sites, chosen for the event. The couple have decided to begin the celebrations the evening before the wedding when their friends arrive in Turin. They will gather in one of the city's oldest restaurants, where our chosen decoration will glorify the stylistic characteristics and colors of the eighteenth-century period rooms. In a true triumph of white and gold paneling, antique crystal lamps, and velvets, the couple will welcome friends and family members in a pleasant celebration in the culinary tradition of Piedmont.

Our imagination is left free of any bonds to expand upon the bride's request for her wedding, to take place the next day. The church overlooking the castle is wrapped in a light mist, a perfect embodiment of the ideal winter atmosphere. The pale-carpeted interior, packed with eighteenth-century shapes and decorations, shines with hundreds of candles, ready to welcome

the arrival of the bride. Also awaiting the beginning of the ceremony is a thirty-member chorus and string orchestra. For cocktails, the site is the antique wine cellar, a vast hall once used for all the phases of winemaking and now the perfect setting for large convivial gatherings. White velvets, whimsical bundles of silver branches, and frozen flowers are the prelude to what the guests will find on their arrival in the halls of the castle for the wedding lunch. The newlyweds and their guests sit in the fresco hall at a long banquet table on which snow, ice, and mirrors play the leading role. With the coming of night, the castle is wrapped in an increasingly thick blanket of fog that only adds to the fairy-tale atmosphere. It is the moment of the cake cutting that seals the evening: It will be served in the wine cellar, transformed yet again for this occasion. Everything shines with silvery lights. The neoclassical façade of the castle, which serves as the background to the first slice, seems to rise from the snow in the light of the moon.

On the eve before their wedding, the couple have organized a dinner in a historic restaurant in Turin to welcome the many guests who arrive early for the event.

In the main rooms of the elegant restaurant, period decorations and furnishings create a special atmosphere.

*The groom wears white gold
Art Deco cufflinks.*

*The bride's gown is made with inserts of precious
Chantilly lace, and the same material is used to
embellish the cushion for the rings.*

A long white runner covers the steps leading to the church; its outer edges are decorated with cushions of baby's breath. Contrasting with the brick façade are two cast-iron vases full of roses, fir branches, and coffee-bush berries resting on modern white lacquer tables. Winter, the theme and season of the event, fills the square in front of the castle with an evocative white mist.

The decorations in the church include a series of elaborate branched candlestands. The cups beneath them are filled with fir, white roses, and coffee bush berries. The composition is completed by spheres of baby's breath placed atop the stands (above and opposite).

The booklet with the texts for the Mass has been personalized with the couple's embossed monogram.

The bride's bouquet is a small natural composition of buttercups, freesia, and white roses. During the Mass, it rests on the prie-dieu near the rings, which are about to be exchanged by the bride and groom.

The interior of the church is illuminated by many candles that shine from the branched candlestands. The softness of asparagus ferns makes the compact arrangements of flowers and berries stand out more sharply.

The reception takes place in the castle, with the table for the wedding party set up in a hall with stuccos and frescoes. Everything recalls and pays homage to winter—the white of the flowers, the berries, the fir branches, the crystals and mirrors, and even the chairs, which have been painted silver for the occasion.

The couple's monogram is embossed on the cover of the menu, which is tied closed with a ribbon sealed with a crystal. It also appears inside the small cones holding rice.

Large columns of baby's breath and white roses decorate the tables in the wine cellar, a space once used for the working of grapes.

Bundles of branches that seem covered with snow rest on white velvet. Among them are groups of antique wooden candleholders.

The wedding cake is an architectural wonder composed of stacked hexagons decorated with white icing on a silver background.

Rhapsody in red

Here is an event that overturns the traditional rules of a wedding. The bride and groom both live in the United States, but she's Italian, and he's English, which makes it difficult to decide where to hold their wedding and which celebrations to organize around it. After reflection, the idea that seems most appealing is to divide the event into two phases. The intimate ceremony, with its deep emotions, will be celebrated on the romantic beach of a small island in the Caribbean. Only the bride and groom and their witnesses will attend.

The big party, however, which will unite members of both families and all their friends, will take place a little later at the family villa overlooking the final stretch of the Ligurian Sea, right on the border with the Côte d'Azur. Here, on a spur of rock stands an unusual neoclassical house that seems to rise from a large semicircular swimming pool and is then reflected in the sea down below.

It is an enchanting site, but its shape presents many challenges. The garden is of considerable size but is divided into numerous smaller spaces in a play of recesses and surprises that open onto one another at different

levels. At the same time, there is the sea, a compelling background that seizes the gaze in every direction.

The plan begins by turning each of these settings into a special locale where the guests can pause. The connecting thread in the preparations is the bride's favorite color, a particular tone of Bordeaux red, which will appear in fabrics, ribbons, and candles, as well as in the thousands and thousands of roses that will decorate the villa.

The music too will change from place to place within the garden, creating different moods throughout the reception.

As soon as darkness falls, a series of lighting maneuvers bring the garden magically to life, revealing new settings for the second part of the evening. In the spot where the guests were received with a welcoming toast, there now appears, as though by magic, a platform for dancing. At the center of this stands a small pavilion reminiscent of the bathing huts of Riviera tradition, that tonight shelters the wedding cake, a sumptuous multilayered construction of icing, spun sugar, and velvety roses. At the instant the cake is cut, fireworks explode and illuminate the bay with thousands of colored lights.

The pool almost seems to blend into the sea beneath it; from this viewpoint, the sky and earth come together in an immense blue embrace.

Enormous floral columns in variations of the chosen shade of red mark off the perimeter of the terrace overlooking the sea.

Set up across the terraces are large candles of Bordeaux red in white containers.

103

On the uppermost terrace is the table with the Bordeaux-red gift boxes for the guests, arranged in a circle around large vases for the presentation of the traditional sugared almonds.

The neoclassically inspired garden is divided into numerous spaces that suddenly open into one another. This suggested the idea of using them to create different atmospheres and moods.

A dramatic pool of water is surrounded by a design in red petals punctuated by candles of the same color.

Groups of sofas and lighting elements decorate every corner of the garden and every terrace of the villa, which, at sunset, is illuminated by candles.

A tall hedge, trimmed into a strict geometric form, is illuminated by cascades of light inserted within the hedge's green arcades.

In the back of the garden is a large gazebo closed off by organza curtains in
Bordeaux red; inside is a table bearing transparent vases filled with red flowers.

As the newlyweds are about to cut the cake, the fireworks display begins,
illuminating the sea and the bay.

The cake appears enclosed in a gazebo whose shape recalls that of the one-time bathing huts used on the Riviera. The cake is decorated with flowers of icing and spun sugar enclosed in a network of coral white.

Reflections of light

he birthplace of the bride or groom is often a determining factor in the selection of sites for a wedding. In this case, both come from Lombardy. The bride grew up on Lake Como; the groom is from Brescia. Their shared tie to the land must be borne in mind as they consider locations, but at first they are unsure—they face a wide range of possibilities, each of which seems inviting. Their shared indecision disappears, though, when they see this dream location, nestled at the foot of the Alps with the Po Valley spreading before it. It is a magical site, between the sky and the earth, between the labor of the fields and spiritual meditation. In fact, it once housed a convent and still preserves the original shape of the small town that grew up around it.

Visible even from a distance, despite the vineyards that surround it, the ancient convent is made up of a series of unusual, highly evocative spaces. There is the panoramic garden with its original porticoes, the protected cloister, and the refectory. There are vaults, arches, columns, and one hall that opens into another, then, suddenly, by way of a narrow passageway, brings you to the surprise within a surprise: the ancient

convent church. A recent restoration has brought it back to new life, transforming it into a perfect space for the reception that will follow the ceremony.

The choice of location having been made, our meetings with the young couple focus on learning about their desires and special dreams for the wedding. Primary importance goes to the bride's passion for precious stones, warm colors, and the shine of crystal. These elements will become the theme of the event.

Equally important to the success of the ceremony is the church where the rite will be held. Neoclassical in style and medium in size, its main altar and side chapels are full of rich decoration. The building stands in the upper part of the town and is reached by way of a long stairway built of stones from the river, which evokes the idea of a pale carpet of apparently endless extent. This will be flanked by lengths of interwoven ivy, jasmine, honeysuckle, and silk ribbons.

At the entrance to the church, the shadowy interior welcomes the guests and accentuates the light from the rows of hanging candlelit lanterns casting their glow onto floral combinations that match the white of baby's breath with roses.

The bride's principal request, an arrangement full of shininess and crystals, remains to be satisfied; it will appear in the décor at the next location. With the fall of evening, the party crosses the cloister, brought to life by colorful fabric and flowers, to the entrance of what was originally the church, now transformed into a place dedicated to the most worldly of rites and glorious with the reflections of mirrors and crystals. The culmination of the celebrations? The wedding cake, decorated with hundreds of gemstones.

The final touches to the bride's elaborate hairstyle, which makes the most of her long, golden tresses.

The bridesmaids hold simple garlands of woven ivy.

The church where the ceremony will take place stands at the center of the small town. The building's façade is softened by neoclassical citations. The main portal is embellished (opposite) with a rich frame of roses, lisianthus, jasmine, and ivy, emphasizing tones of white and pink.

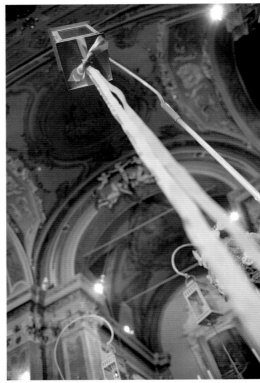

The narrow path to the altar has been decorated with suspended candlelight
lanterns (above) and flower balls made with baby's breath wrapped
with spirals of roses, white lisianthus, and small silk butterflies of
delicate pink color (opposite).

At first deliberately left uncovered, the floor was strewn with white rose petals
just before the arrival of the bride.

The colors chosen for the ceremony recur in a series of details, from the straw bags carried by the bridesmaids to the sugared almonds, from the fabrics of the cushions to the small floral bouquets.

Delicate sachets in transparent pale pink organza hold the rice for the traditional good-luck salute at the end of the nuptial ceremony.

The outer garden has been furnished with arrangements of small tables and white sofas to comfortably accommodate the many guests. The sheltered inner cloister is more in keeping with the layout of an Italian garden: A thick hedge forms a green space that makes the white architecture, decorated with the pink panels draped between the arches, stand out.

Cushions scattered among the cloister arches offer comfortable spots for the guests to rest and converse. The decoration of this large space is dominated by long panels of organza alternating with rows of ribbons from which small mirrors sway in the breeze, reflecting and flashing light.

A small oval silk box containing a little surprise has been prepared for each guest (above). The napkin, wrapped around the menu, is embellished by a ribbon and a brooch in stones and crystals, elements that were also chosen for the design of the guests' tables (above and opposite).

What was formerly a church is now a dining room. The round tables have been arranged to seat eight to ten people. Illuminated by beams of light from above, the tables shine with their decorations of crystal, mirrors, flowers, and candles.

A book of poems, closed with a ribbon held tight by an almond, is the souvenir that each guest receives at the end of the wedding.

The fabric pavilion set up for the cutting of the cake is illuminated by the soft light of many small suspended lanterns. This moment is the high point of the reception. The cake pays homage to the bride's love of gems: With patience and skill, the chef has made a fantastic construction of icing encrusted with colored crystals.

With nightfall, the façade of the ancient convent takes on new grace through the skilled application of lighting. To emphasize the magic of the evening, the leaves of the trees in the garden are illuminated by candles lit inside small lanterns.

The emotions of Venice

*I*t's a true challenge, the one presented by this young couple. The idea is full of charm, but pulling it off will be anything but easy. The problems begin with the main characters, a pair of brilliant professionals. They have precious little time to dedicate to the preparation of their wedding, and what's more—not a negligible detail—they live in Los Angeles. Their families are in New York and Chicago. The ceremony will take place far from everyone's home, in Venice, and calls for three days of celebrations and parties.

The solution to the first problem—how to welcome the guests on their arrival in Venice—is almost immediate. What better way than by offering them Venice's famous cocktails in St. Mark's Square, right under the arches of the Procuratie, in the most beautiful drawing room in Europe, with the background accompaniment of outdoor orchestras. This immediately immerses the guests in the magical atmosphere that will remain with them for the three days dedicated to the event. The next day, following American tradition, is the rehearsal, after which they dine together in the historical Pisani-Moretta Palace overlooking the Grand Canal.

The wedding itself will be a Jewish ceremony, so a *huppah*, the traditional tent representing the celestial vault, is set up in the historical garden of the Hotel Cipriani. Under the *huppah*, with its covering of festoons interwoven with white flowers, the bride and groom exchange vows. The romantic background of the lagoon is splendid in the Venetian light. At the conclusion of the ceremony, the guests are led along a typical Venetian *calle* to the opposite side of the Giudecca for cocktails before the astonishing backdrop of the basin of St. Mark's. For the occasion the doors of the Granaries of the Venetian Republic have been opened. This long, narrow space with high walls suggests the use of two banquet tables, and these are decorated in tones of white and lavender. The scenographic play of light inside this historic work of architecture highlights the building's original brick and wooden-beamed structure. As evening falls Venice is once again the perfect magical setting for the ceremonial cutting of the cake and the wedding toasts. And the few minutes the guests have spent on the street outside the granaries are time enough for the stage to be transformed. As though by enchantment, the furnishings change, the dinner tables are swept away, and different floral decorations arrive. This new and unexpected space is ready to welcome the guests to a night of partying. It is a final *coup de théâtre* worthy of the fabled magnificence of the Serenissima.

Everything is ready for the ceremony. The huppah, draped with floral garlands, stands out against the background of the lagoon, while the orchestra awaits the start of the event. A carpet of white rose petals has been spread for the bride's passage. The guests will sit on small armchairs covered in white fabric, with a copy of the booklet for the ceremony on each seat.

The bride's bouquet is a small bunch of lilies in shades of pink. This is the only such note of color amid all the floral arrangements, which are dominated by white flowers and the green of foliage.

The tones of white and green presented by hydrangea, viburnum, and buttercups are the chromatic theme chosen for the boutonnieres that will be given to the guests as well as for the sumptuous decorations in the antique iron vases arranged alongside the canal.

As a prelude to the actual wedding cake, there are many small cakes in pastry flour and icing (right).

Each of the long banquet tables is identified by a
simple card bearing a Roman numeral. At each
place setting, the name of the guest is written on
a ribbon of transparent organza wrapped around
the menu.

A long mirror runs the full length of the table, reflecting an apparent infinity of candles alternating with transparent vases of white flowers and, here and there, a note of lilac. Panels of organza have been suspended from the ceiling to break up the great height of the hall, and from them dangle spiraling ribbons.

The wedding cake—made in New York—arrives by plane before dinner; the decoration must be arranged on the spot in Venice and is a triumph of spiraling sugar blossoms (below).

Boxes made of icing contain white and lilac candies (left). At bottom left is a display of the seating arrangement for the dinner.

The moment for the celebration has arrived. The hall, transformed as though by magic while the guests were attending the cutting of the cake, is now dedicated to music and dance. Even the flowers have been changed: To warm the setting, preference has gone to tints of Bordeaux and vivid reds, tones that are accentuated by the glow of the candles.

Naturally lilac

*P*assion for the color lilac is the thread connecting all the decisions made for the organization of this wedding. The couple, *amanti* of travel and art, are in search of a locale combining the kind of atmosphere that only nature can provide with the increased intimacy of ancient sites. They are looking for a theatrical backdrop for the wedding as well as a spot suited to the full weekend of celebrations planned with their family and friends. The choice falls on Bormio, in the heart of Lombardy's Alps. A small church, with the simplicity of stone and wood, will be the site of the ceremony. The celebrations will take place at a historic hotel, formerly the royal residence during the hunting season. All that remains is to do everything possible to satisfy the bride's desires. This begins with decorating the church, which will be entered by way of a small wood-framed door surrounded by flowering climbing plants. Inside, the guests will witness the ceremony from beneath a symphony of flowers in pale shades of lilac, pink, and white suspended in fir-wood baskets. From there, they will travel through the grassy fields that have already taken on the colors of autumn to the Grand Hotel. For the occasion, the big antique

door built to accommodate guests arriving in carriages will be opened. Once again the palette of colors will be that requested by the couple, exalted by a magical play of lights that will reach its culmination in the sumptuous dining room. Here the bride will change bouquets, now wearing a sphere of minuscule buds suspended from her wrist on a silk ribbon—lilac, naturally. After the aperitif the guests will enter the majestic hall where they will be entertained during dinner by the music of a chamber orchestra.

A sitting room has been prepared for the cutting of the cake. The tables are covered in moss, illuminated by candlelight; the air is saturated by a white cloud pierced by shafts of light that point to the cloud of tulle that hides the wedding cake. Music and dancing will go on through the night.

The chromatic theme for the wedding is lilac; thus, it appears in the light and discreet touches in the bride's outfit, as well as the groom's tie and boutonniere.

The interior of the church is somewhat spartan, with traces of fresco in faded colors along the walls. The decoration is concentrated on the altar, which is heaped with woven arrangements of fir, roses, dahlias, and lisianthus. Fir-wood baskets hang from above on lilac silk ribbons and contain baby's breath, roses, and dahlias.

For the wedding ceremony, the altar has been embellished with a garland of fir boughs and large lit candles.

The bride's bouquet, resting on a velvet prie-dieu during the ceremony, is a small composition of roses, heather, and woodland berries bound with a silk band.

141

The hotel dining room chosen for the reception is an elegant, beautifully decorated setting that dates to the end of the nineteenth century. The table at the center has been prepared for the bride and groom and their closest friends.

The fountain in front of the hotel is illuminated by a beam of colored light.

Every corner of the hotel's halls has been richly decorated with candlestands, bowls of sugared almonds, and flowers in the tones of lilac, pink, and fuchsia.

A special milky fog, created for the occasion, fills the room with the perfume of the woods, then disperses to reveal the cake. It is a many-tiered creation of red currants, blackberries, raspberries, and blueberries. The tables, covered in moss, are illuminated by candles.

Between art and nature

Salento, a splendid land of olive trees and rolling fields criss-crossed with stone walls, where the Adriatic and Ionian seas meet: This is the splendid, unspoiled setting where this wedding will take place. The bride and groom, both strongly tied to their origins, want their wedding to glorify and embellish an area so profoundly marked by nature and by art. They propose the butterfly as the unifying theme for their celebration. But which church should they use for the event, and which palace should they choose from among the many that crowd the area, all magnificent? The large number of guests eliminates the smaller churches, and in the end the choice falls on a medium-size church that is a splendid example of the Lecce baroque. The decision is made to decorate each of the altars, which look like delicate works of engraved stone, with a cascade of greenery and flowers. Age-old olive trees line the route taken by the newlyweds, who will be welcomed as they exit the ceremony by a flight of butterflies released for the occasion into the glowing, cloudless June sky.

After visiting several noble palaces in the area, the choice of where to hold the party falls on the ducal palace of Lopez y Royo. At first glance,

the building, which overlooks an old park, seems to be in a compromised state of preservation. In recent years nature has more or less taken over the garden. But those very characteristics, combined with the opportunity to carry out restoration work that will return the place to its former appearance, are inspiration enough to take on the challenge.

A combination farm and manor house, the historic palace faces the road with an elegant façade. For the occasion, the road will be closed to traffic and completely covered by a long runner. A more rustic façade looks onto a magnificent terrace of about a thousand square meters. This will be the site for the cocktails; guests will travel paths of beaten earth lined by palms, pines, and orange trees to reach the site organized for dinner. The garden, restored and conserved before the event, will be brought back to life. It will transport the guests back to a distant time when the dukes used it for receptions. The tennis court is turned into a dining room with the installation of a fabric pavilion capable of seating six hundred guests. The oldest part of the garden, sheltered by a majestic ancient oak, will be the site for the cutting of the wedding cake. Here, beneath a profusion of flowers forming enormous garlands hanging from the branches of the big tree, the newlyweds will toast their joy, cutting a composition of icing and flowers to the accompaniment of an orchestra.

*Wearing a veil bordered in antique lace, the
bride makes her entrance against the majestic
background of the baroque church door.*

The sumptuous church interior is a splendid example
of the Lecce baroque, with a play of contrasts
among the altars. For the wedding, these are richly
decorated with festoons woven of greenery and
flowers, and the nave is filled with olive trees
wrapped in tulle.

The fringe of the prie-dieux and the hassocks of the
bride and groom rest softly on the grass carpet.

Each of the male guests has received a pair of colorful personalized socks to wear on the day of the wedding.

A corner of the palace garden is set up with cushions and lanterns and transformed into an appealing spot for conversation.

Every table is decorated with a garland of Pittosporum, roses, and lisianthus over which hover small organza butterflies, the chosen emblem of the wedding.

The tables, arranged on the tennis court, are set with transparent chairs decorated with lilac cushions.

*The age-old oak is richly
decorated with large garlands
bursting with roses, peonies,
and lisianthus.*

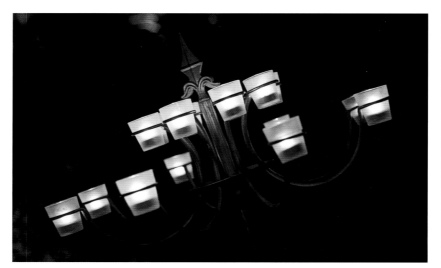

The cake is a triumph of white chocolate on which rest butterflies in white icing.

Ceremony in the fields

The request for this wedding plan came from New York. From so far away, the bride and groom asked for suggestions for a place where they could have their ceremony and, at the same time, host all the friends and family members who would arrive for the occasion. The wedding itself would represent a union of hearts and cultures: The groom is American, and the bride, of Chinese ancestry, brings with her some of the traditions tied to her family's culture, which often influence the choice of the day, the site, or other details of a wedding.

After evaluating proposals from all over Italy, the bride and groom ultimately select Tuscany. In particular, they would like to rent a magnificent villa where they can spend a week together with their closest friends. The organizing team moves with them to the site to prepare.

Part of the ceremony is the traditional dinner that will precede the day of the event. The decision is made to hold this at the Piccolomini Palace in Pienza. Here, the guests will be offered cocktails during a party celebrating the reunion of friends from all over the world. The sunset behind the hills illuminates the palace's magnificent Italian-style garden, its

pathways filled with strolling guests. For this occasion, the bride wears a dress with inserts of red lace, a touch of Chinese tradition. The next day the villa in which the couple and their guests are staying is transformed for the big event. The natural setting is enchanting; the barren hills that roll on and on as far as the eye can see are almost lunar.

For the ceremony itself, an altar is constructed directly on the grass, enclosed in the embrace of greenery and tulle, with the setting sun as its backdrop.

The guests take their seats in chairs set up in rows and watch as the bride, wearing a dress of white lace, moves with her bridesmaids toward the gazebo. Violins and a harp accompany the progress and mark off the important moments of the celebration, which ends with a round of applause honoring the joy of the newlyweds. Now comes the more informal moment of the cocktails. After the emotion of the ceremony, everyone enjoys the atmosphere that surrounds the villa.

With nightfall the guests take their places at a single horseshoe-shaped table set up around a body of water that seems to flow toward infinity. The bride takes her place at the elaborate table on which flowers are surrounded by flights of many small white butterflies. She now wears a red dress, the color of good luck, and with her husband she watches as the thousands of lights of the fireworks illuminate the night.

The series of dresses that the bride will wear: The red dress is destined for the evening finale.

The ceremony is about to begin, and the bridesmaids help the bride with the final touches to her dress.

The dress chosen for the ceremony is a romantic creation in lace that will be followed over the course of the celebrations by two others.

The gazebo where the ceremony will take place, delicately framed by spirals of asparagus fern, has as backdrop a fantasy landscape of hills and trees. The composition on the altar is made up of roses, carnations, and peonies.

The bride's bouquet is a delicate arrangement of sweet-pea blossoms enclosed in a band of lilac-colored silk.

The bridesmaids bear small bouquets of ivory roses that perfectly complement the lilac sashes of their dresses.

The banquet table surrounds three sides of a body of water and has the villa as its backdrop. Sofas are distributed across the garden, shaded by white fabric canopies.

Distributed along the table are groups of antique wicker baskets containing arrangements of roses and varieties of dianthus over which fly small white butterflies (below, opposite). The background of the menu repeats the decorative motif of the invitations.

The seating plan makes clear to each guest where he or she is to sit.

With the coming of darkness, the flicker of a thousand carefully positioned candles creates a new setting that is completely different from that of the day.

Lantern lights shine from beneath the pergolas.

167

During dinner, without the guests being aware of anything, a small tent is set up from which crystals cascade. The cake reproduces an original from the Victorian era rendered less formal by the addition of flying butterflies.

The cake is a composition with several different-sized levels. Its outer shell of icing encloses a heart of crème chantilly and sponge cake.

Following pages:
The fireworks display sends flashes of bright color into the night sky.

169

Sparkling by the sea

A famous movie and a color related to the movie's title: These make up the request from a couple for the basic themes of their wedding. Indeed, the two have already chosen the location, a beautiful park on the hill of Posillipo overlooking the Mediterranean, near the house where they will live together. Not far off is the church, which is impressive and austere, distinguished most of all by a wonderful stairway that leads to the church courtyard. The first conversation with the couple brings to light their passion for the film *Breakfast at Tiffany's* and, from there, the request for that special color known as Tiffany blue. A visit to the church makes clear the theatrical force of that stairway and the courtyard surrounded by pale marble, which contrasts with the multicolor Vietri ceramics of the interior church floor. The eventual plan for the wedding includes using floral decorations and accessories to bring the exterior of the church to life. The guests will line up there to watch the bride, wearing a splendid gown custom made in Paris, ascend to the church amid clouds of flowers and candles in elaborate holders.

And next, how to transform an outdoor space dedicated to relaxation

into a site suitable for a reception? The answer is the installation of a transparent tensile structure to house the dinner, along with carpets, cushions, and sofas for the period preceding the dinner and for the party to follow. The guests can move freely between the exterior and interior, between the covered and the open areas, that wonderful panorama always in view. We wonder how to apply the chosen theme—until the sea itself comes to our aid with its glinting reflections and its colors at sunset. We decide to amplify these effects with hundreds of crystals suspended over the tables to reflect the candlelight. The banquet tables display constant notes of Tiffany blue contrasting with the pale tones of the linens and the flowers. As evening falls, the park fills with new light at the appearance of the cake, a triumph of pale hearts against a background of icing that is, naturally, the right shade of blue. An embrace of organza encloses the couple during their wedding toast in a scene dominated by a splendid full moon.

The bride wears an exclusive haute couture *gown from Paris.*

On her father's arm the bride ascends the stairway and crosses the marble terrace toward the church where the wedding ceremony will take place.

Dressed in morning coats, the best man and the ushers await the arrival of the bride at the entrance to the church.

The white marble balustrade that encloses the space of the altar has been decorated with soft cushions of baby's breath, white roses, lisianthus, and dahlias.

At the conclusion of the ceremony, the newlyweds lead the guests out of the church and down the all-important stairway, decorated for the occasion with a pale runner.

The panorama from the hill of Posillipo takes in the Gulf of Naples, a blue expanse tinged with the shades of sunset.

Each guest receives a place card indicating his or her seat at the long tables.

The banquet tables are dressed with white flowers that alternate with fabric boxes used as decorative elements. Chains of crystals hang from above.

The menu uses different colors for the presentation of each serving and is accompanied by a blown-glass cylinder full of sugared almonds.

Suspended over the tables are large garlands composed of interwoven fabric, crystal chains, and inserts of white flowers, all illuminated by candlelight.

It's time for the party in the garden overlooking the sea. The garden has been furnished with sofas, large carpets, and white cushions arranged under the Scotch pines.

The cake peeks from behind transparent silk organza—it is an embroidery of sugar curls in which sweet hearts seem to take flight.

Countryside elegance

Children are not usually enthusiastic participants in a wedding, but in this case children were given the entire day for their games. One of them, the son of the bridal couple, played a leading role; he even received his baptism during the wedding ceremony. For the occasion, the relatives and friends were invited to the family villa in the splendid Tuscan hills of Siena. It was a sunny day, and the small private chapel, hidden among olive trees, was dressed up for the ceremony. On the outside, flowering plants in an ensemble of antique country baskets made the entrance to the little church even more inviting; inside, rows of suspended baskets enlivened the setting with notes of white. The chosen flower for the event was chamomile. On the wedding day it softly spilled from containers made of natural materials hanging from iron rods. The bride, wearing an elegant short dress, crossed fields and olive groves to reach the chapel where her son and his father awaited her.

The ceremony begins. The guests must listen in from outside: So small is the church that there is room only for the couple and the witnesses. The ceremony concludes, as scheduled, at a late-morning hour, and everyone

An old restructured country house, the couple's summer residence, will host the reception for a double celebration, the marriage of the couple and the baptism of their child.

relocates to the garden of the villa, where cocktails are served. When the time comes to sit down and eat, there is another surprise. The site chosen for the meal is the pool. Its rectangular shape has suggested the idea of a single, large table extending all around it. Chamomile flowers appear in profusion along the full length of the table. They have been put in vases, tucked into the silver cups that are to be souvenirs for the guests, and hand-painted on the menus at each person's place setting. The guests have been given white umbrellas to protect them in case of rain, but this turns out to be a fine, very warm day; the umbrellas are transformed into parasols. The celebration is about to reach its height, and for the cutting of the cake—in this case, many cakes—everyone returns to the garden where a table has been set up. It is covered with sweets in a variety of shapes and colors, to the joy of the many children on hand, who rush forward to play around the newlyweds during the delightfully informal wedding toasts.

The bride's bouquet combines antique roses and rosemary; for the baby there is a hand-embroidered christening gown.

The ceremony takes place in the estate's private chapel surrounded by olive trees. The exterior is softened by a collection of flowering plants in antique baskets. An old container for bulbs has been reinvented as a holder for cones filled with rice to be thrown when the newlyweds leave the chapel.

The interior decoration of the small church is composed of groups of baskets bursting with chamomile and baby's breath interspersed with small globes of blown glass; just before the bride's entrance, the floor of the chapel is covered with a thick carpet of rose petals.

Every corner of the house and garden has been decorated with small silk sacks filled with roses, dahlias, and mulberries.

The pool becomes the centerpiece of the seating arrangement, which calls for a continuous table around its perimeter and decorations of white and green.

Chamomile flowers decorate the table and are painted on each menu, joined to a napkin by a green silk ribbon.

Silver cups filled with white roses serve as place markers for the guests.

Concern about the possibility of showers prompted the creation of personalized white umbrellas, but the nearly cloudless, warm day calls for them to be used as parasols.

Elegant silk boxes contain a selection of small colored candies.

In homage to the many children taking part in the celebration, several cakes have been made in different shapes and colors to serve as frames to the wedding cake.

The icing presents a variety of shapes colored in delicate tints; once again, chamomile flowers are the symbol of the event.

As white as snow

An intimate ceremony, only relatives and close friends, in a site full of memories and emotions—this is the point of departure that the couple propose, adding that we will have little time, no more than a month, to put everything together. The chosen site is Alagna, a mountain locale at the foot of Monte Rosa; the Walser culture of nearby Switzerland can be felt strongly there. Passionate about mountain sports, the bride and groom have always spent their vacations at this spot, and so their wedding must be there, too. They have rented an entire hotel for the occasion. The ceremony will take place in the splendid parish church, its interior full of carved wooden altars decorated in the style typical of Valsesian art.

For the occasion, the bride has chosen a dress made with a mixture of wool and light silk and wears, in place of the traditional veil, a matching bonnet. The wedding will be celebrated during the evening Mass, so the couple will be surrounded not only by their family and guests but by all the residents of the village. The choice of color—snow white—appears in the church decorations in the exterior and the interior and is highlighted with

interwoven pale flowers, woodland berries, and fir boughs. Upon their exit from the church, the wedding party is met by fires lit for the preparation of mulled wine, creating a moment of great conviviality.

The colors of the floral decorations change inside the hotel chosen for the reception: Warm wool and velvets become the dominant theme. For the dinner, a single large table is set up at which the couple can sit with their guests. Large vases covered in fir, flowers in the tonalities of Bordeaux and violet, and woodland berries are arranged along a rift of snow crystals that covers the velvet of the table. At the end of the dinner, the guests descend to more intimate rooms overlooking the river. There, amid a fantastic arrangement of snowy branches, they find the wedding cake. Once again, woolen yarns are featured in the artisanal decorations, worked with skill into snowflakes. The guests are then led onto the outer terrace where, as though by magic, the woods and waterfall below are brought to vivid life by a fireworks display arranged for the couple.

The illuminated portico in front of the church stands out against the background of Monte Rosa. The decoration here, a prelude to that of the interior, is composed of garlands of fir and woodland berries alternating with flowered spheres.

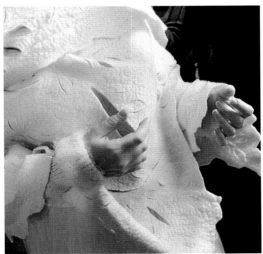

The bride's gown is an homage to the mountain: precious wools and artisanal fabrics.

The church is distinguished by its impressive wooden altar. Free of any decoration that might hide its beauty, it serves as the ideal background for rows of fir garlands and white flowers. All the balustrades of the side chapels are decorated with fir, roses, lisianthus, and candles (opposite).

Outside the church, fires have been lit to prepare mulled wine for the guests.

A single table is set up for the dinner, its dominant color, shades of Bordeaux red. Tulips, anemones, hyacinths, buttercups, and roses are gathered in vases of fir boughs and dogwood, alternating with long candles in glass holders.

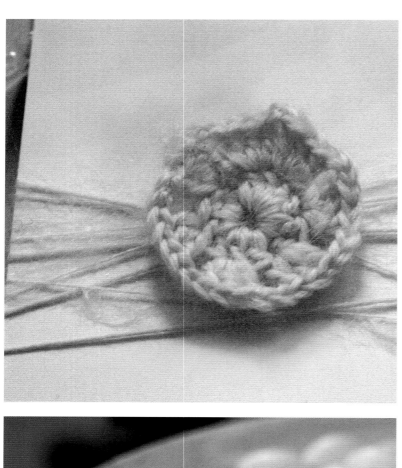

The menu and the wedding cake are decorated with interwoven woolen yarns forming flowers and stylized snowflakes.

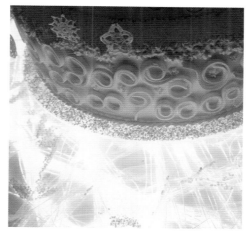

The cake is enclosed in an arrangement of branches from which dangle small glass candleholders. At the moment the cake is cut, the wooden bridge over the waterfall outside is illuminated by a beautiful display of shining light.

Rustic inspiration

The setting is the beautiful countryside around one of the most famous towns in Tuscany; the chosen wedding site is the family villa, surrounded by a well-tended flowering garden and vineyards. The site is absolute perfection; the difficulty is the sheer embarrassment of riches in terms of choosing where to stage the various scenes of the wedding. Our solution is to create a kind of itinerant event, guiding the guests to a variety of places so they can fully enjoy their beauty.

The ceremony, simple and with only a few guests in attendance, takes place at the city hall, offering those present a moment of intimacy before the large-scale celebrations begin. The flawless weather shows off the magnificent natural setting to its fullest, and the many guests gather in the villa's garden, which has been arranged to create an open-air living room.

When lunchtime arrives, the guests are led to a nearby field alongside a magnificent old farmhouse. Here a pavilion has been set up completely covered in lengths of raw linen, a structure like those erected for courtly receptions during the Renaissance. The long table is covered in natural linen richly decorated with a hand-embroidered floral motif; the napkins,

which bear the monogram of the bride and groom, are positioned near white fans, also personalized, part of the table setting for each guest. The plates are artisan ceramics made for the occasion, and each is accompanied by a piece of colored blown-glass stemware that the guests are invited to keep as souvenirs of the day.

The arrangement is an explosion of nature: garlands of straw, wicker baskets bursting with seasonal flowers and vegetables, woodland berries, and bouquets of chamomile and aromatic herbs.

A veritable symphony of perfumes, flavors, and colors welcomes and embraces the couple and their guests as they dine in the shade of the tent. When it comes time for the cake, they return to the villa. There, in the most shaded and secluded area of the garden, an airy gazebo of tulle surrounds the magnificent multitiered cake. As evening begins to fall, the lights of torches and lanterns come on, as well as many floating islands of light in the pool, creating the background for a night of partying.

A basket of silk sachets full of the scents of the country and supplies for lovers of toscano cigars have been provided for the guests.

Rustic ceramics and blown-glass vases decorate the tables presenting the sugared-almond favors.

The many decorative motifs include garlands of straw interwoven with box tree and lanterns suspended along the outside of the pavilion.

The wedding plan calls for creation of a fabric pavilion as the site of the luncheon. The linen used has been artisan-printed with decorative motifs. Its soft draping provides the background for garlands of straw and box tree embellished with linen ribbons.

Garlands of straw and box tree, baskets of flowers and woodland berries, cascades of ornamental tomatoes—and visible in the background is the tablecloth of embroidered natural linen.

On the lunch table, traditional loaves of bread alternate with baskets
of flowers and vegetables.

The place setting for each guest includes a fan, a colored glass offered
as a souvenir, and a small gift of aromatic herbs, a little piece of the
Tuscan countryside.

Chamomile, asparagus, and eggplant are among the elements of the natural compositions that decorate the entire table.

The row of green ceramic plates echoes the row of baskets full of natural products on the table.

The pavilion for the lunch has been set up at the
center of a vineyard alongside an antique farmhouse.

The cake awaits the guests in the innermost garden, under a veil of tulle.

The party is enlivened by a multitude of
scenographic lights. By now it is night, and
the pool is illuminated with an archipelago
of floating candles.

Masked invitation

*T*he chosen site is the incomparable stage of the city of Venice, which by itself presents hosts of ideas that unleash the imagination. It is a great setting for a great event, too important to be contained within a single day. Three days are to be packed with celebrations, beginning with subdued tones and rising in a crescendo to become a symphony of enrapturing emotions. The first evening is dedicated to the reception of the guests, who arrive from all over the world. This takes place in the historic setting of Café Florian, transformed for the occasion into a private salon. The second day, the evening of the wedding celebration, sees all the guests collected around the couple for a gala dinner event. Rooms in a palazzo overlooking the Grand Canal have been chosen as the site for this sophisticated evening. The richly frescoed ceiling of the great salon suggests decorations using warm tones: purple, Bordeaux, and the most intense reds alternate and blend in the bursts of colorful flowers in over-size blown-glass vases placed on the many tables arranged around the hall. The third day provides the triumphant conclusion to this magical event, by way of a truly dramatic performance in two acts. The wedding

ceremony is in the morning, and for the occasion the rooms of a historic home are opened: This is the central hall, or portego, of the Pisani-Moretta Palace. The couple and their guests arrive by way of the canal, entering through the waterside door to witness the rite. Minuets and famous tunes by Vivaldi echo through the salons and create a musical background for the solemn moment.

The second act—a magnificent masked ball—takes place in the evening. The sumptuous rooms of the *piano nobile* at the Pisani-Moretta Palace are opened, illuminated by hundreds of candles set in antique Murano candlestands.

"Moors" in eighteenth-century costume bearing large fans of white feathers welcome the guests and lead them up the grand stairway. All wear costumes suited to the period, as well as splendid masks. A long banquet table has been set for dinner. Shining across its length is antique silverware bearing the heraldic arms of the palace. The delicate décor is of the purest white. Against a background of frescoes, the newlyweds bring to a conclusion the many festivities with the cutting of the cake.

For the bouquet, preference was given to a composition using small lilies and Galax leaves.

The couple make their way beneath the porticoes of the Procuratie in St. Mark's Square and will soon arrive at the historical Café Florian to welcome their guests with cocktails.

The ceiling fresco inspired the colors of the floral decorations for the hall that will be the site of the gala dinner the evening before the wedding.

Compositions of roses, lisianthus, lilac, and Symphoricarpos berries fill the blown-glass vases of different heights arranged on the tables, each of which has been given the name of a palace or important site in Venice.

On the day of the wedding, the main salons are opened in the Pisani-Moretta Palace on the Grand Canal.

The ceremony takes place in the portego, accessible from the water door opening onto the Grand Canal. The bride and groom will take their places on chairs beneath an arch of white flowers.

231

The bride's theatrical hairstyle and shimmering gown are for the great masked ball in the salons of the palace.

*The main salon, the gallery of the Pisani-Moretta Palace,
is ablaze in the glitter of antique chandeliers and candles.*

The guests wear sumptuous period costumes that bring to life the past glamour of Venetian festivities.

The banquet table is set with rare pieces of antique
silverware engraved with the heraldic emblems
of the palace.

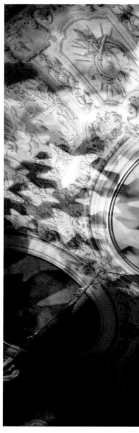

During dinner, musicians alternate with costumed performers singing period pieces, while a group of "Moors," bearing large feather fans, take up positions at the entrance to the salon.

A group of waiters, also in costume, carry the gold-leafed wedding cake to the table, while the ceiling fresco is transformed into a fantastic, swirling starry sky.

Photographic sources

All the photographs in this book are by Massimiliano Morlotti with the following exceptions:
Giuseppe Simone Bartolucci: 74–85, 146, 184
Granataimages, Milan / Almay: / © Tibor Bognar 127; / © Ian Fraser 39
Giovanni Izzo: 174–183
Marka, Milan: / Danilo Donadoni 199 / Walter Zerla 137
Simephoto, Milan: / Peter Adams 75 / Guido Baviera 147; /
© Johanna Huber 223 / Massimo Ripiani 87, 101, 113, 173, 209; /
Giovanni Simeone 51, 185; / Riccardo Spila 27
Tipsimages, Milan / G.A. Rossi 63